Outwit

Make believe

Mischief

Joke

Impossible

NO LONGER PROPERTY OF SEATTLE PUBLIC LIBRARY

Tricky

deceiving

Dodgy

Genius

Hoax

*Weaving spells*

Strange

Knack

*Wizardry*

*Crafty*

Imagination

Scientific

Know – how

*Magic*

Dreaming

Cunning

Mock

Doublecross

Hoodwink

Unreal

Technique

*Shock*

Pretend

False

*Fantasy*

Funny business

P9-CKF-170

# LOOK!

## Really Smart Art

**Gillian Wolfe**

F

FRANCES LINCOLN
CHILDREN'S BOOKS

# To Theresa and Mortimer Sackler

## PHOTOGRAPHIC ACKNOWLEDGMENTS

For permission to reproduce the works of art on the following pages and for supplying images, the Publishers would like to thank:

akg-images: 17, 32–3, 36–7 (© The Estate of Roy Lichtenstein/DACS 2009)
Photograph © The Art Institute of Chicago: 16 (Wirt. D. Walker Fund, 1949.585)
The Art Institute of Chicago/The Bridgeman Art Library: 26–7
© Salvador Dali, Gala-Salvador Dali Foundation, DACS, London 2009: cover (detail) and 30–31
By permission of the Trustees of Dulwich Picture Gallery, London: back cover and 14–15
© 2009 The M.C. Escher Company-Holland. All rights reserved. www.mcescher.com: 8–9
© David Hockney: 12–13 (photo Richard Schmidt)
©Akiyoshi Kitaoka: 39
© Manchester Art Gallery/The Bridgeman Art Library: 10–11
Digital image © 2009, The Museum of Modern Art/Scala, Florence: 18–19 (Acquired through
the Lillie P. Bliss Bequest. 275.1949/© ADAGP, Paris and DACS, London 2009)
Digital image © 2009, The Museum of Modern Art/Scala, Florence: 20–21
(The Sidney and Harriet Janis Collection. 337.1967/© The Pollock-Krasner Foundation ARS, NY and DACS, London 2009)
National Gallery of Australia, Canberra: 25 (© estate of the artist licensed by Aboriginal Artists Agency 2009)
© 2009, The National Gallery, London/Scala, Florence: 22–3
(Bought with a special grant and other contributions, 1959. Accession number 1617)
© Octavio Ocampo: 34–5
Whitney Museum of American Art, New York: 28-9 (gift of the artist. 69.154. photo Sheldan C. Collins)

*Look! Really Smart Art* copyright © Frances Lincoln Limited 2010
Text copyright © Gillian Wolfe 2010

First published in Great Britain and the USA in 2010 by
Frances Lincoln Children's Books, 4 Torriano Mews,
Torriano Avenue, London NW5 2RZ

www.franceslincoln.com

All rights reserved

ISBN: 978-1-84780-010-7

Set in Garamond and Balance

Printed in Shenzhen, Guangdong, China by C&C Offset Printing in April 2010

1 3 5 7 9 8 6 4 2

# Contents

# *Look* – THE 3D TRICK

How does an artist drawing on flat paper make something look **solid**? What makes these hands look real enough to touch? Can you work out how it's done?

The two shirt cuffs are drawn only as outlines. They look completely flat.

## Then the artist's magic begins: out of the flat cuffs appear hands that are shaded

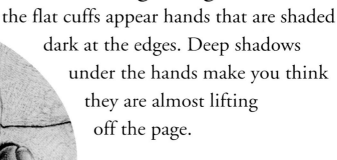

dark at the edges. Deep shadows under the hands make you think they are almost lifting off the page.

Shading helps to **model** a drawing into something **solid** and more real-looking. Even the piece of paper has been drawn to look as if it's pinned to a surface – but this is another clever trick.

Draw your own finger in outline. Then darken the edges to make it look solid, like the fingers in Escher's drawing.

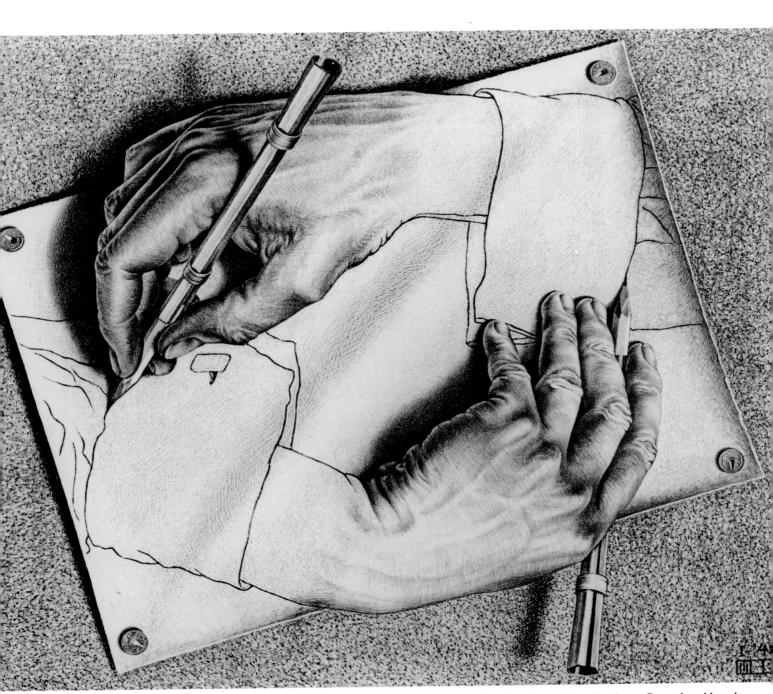

Maurits Cornelius Escher, *Drawing Hands*

Artists have all kinds of inventive ways of showing you how
to see things differently. Turn the pages of this book and
**discover some of their secrets.**

# Look – high speed

Have you ever watched horses racing? When a horse gallops, its powerful back legs push its body forward. Then its front legs thud down on the ground and its back legs kick off again.

Look closely at these horses. Do you notice anything odd?

Alexander von Wagner, *The Chariot Race*

They're flying through the air with all four legs off the ground at the *same time!* The artist knew perfectly well that horses can't possibly do that, so why did he paint it?

He is trying to solve a big problem for artists: how to show **speed of movement.** A film camera can do it, but when drawing and painting on a flat surface, it is far more difficult.

Try drawing an animal
moving fast, or a bird taking
off in flight.

A spectacular chariot race like this actually happened in Ancient Rome.
You can see it in the film *Ben Hur.* We don't mind the artist tricking us
because the effect of the horses pounding towards us is so thrilling.

# *Look* – **near** and far...

**This painting is flat.** So how does the artist make you think that the road is winding *uphill* and *further away* from you until it disappears altogether?

As it winds into the distance, the road narrows. Where the road ends, it comes to a thin, sharp point. This is called 'the vanishing point' because it **vanishes** on the horizon line, where land meets sky.

Drawing things to make them look further away is called using *perspective*. To understand perspective drawing, you just need to remember that things near you are big and things further away from you gradually get smaller.

Eighteen tall trees line the road in this painting. Can you see how the tallest three trees are the ones nearest to you? The others become smaller going down the road. This makes you *think* they are further away. But they're not really, are they?

Try drawing a road
that disappears on the horizon,
with trees on either side that get
smaller along the way.

12

David Hockney, *Going up Garroby Hill*

# L*oo*k – I'm watching you!

## The eyes of someone in a portrait can't move.
Or can they?

Look hard at the beautiful eyes of the young man. He seems to **stare** right back at you.

Now move to one side. Is the man still staring at you? Move to the other side. Is he still staring? You will find that wherever you go in the room, he will *always* be watching you.

This happens because the painting is **flat**. If you move around, you don't see the side of the man's face – but you still see both eyes, and they keep looking your 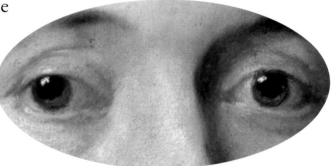 way. This feeling of being watched makes you think how **lifelike** the portrait is. The artist knew that this special *eye contact* would help you remember the face in the painting.

Draw a full face with wide open eyes. Make the centre of the eye – the pupil – round and dark. Now see how the face looks straight back at you.

Isaac Fuller, *Portrait of a Man*

15

# Look —as *real* as can be

We believe what our eyes tell us. You might think that this is a silk curtain hanging in front of a painting of flowers. Look closer. There is nothing real about the curtain. It's all paint!

The French name for paintings that fool your eye is *trompe l'oeil* (pronounced 'tromp-loy') – it means 'deceive the eye'. Another name once used for this type of Dutch painting is 'Little Trickster'.

Adriaen van der Spelt and Frans Mieris, *Still life with a Flower Garland and a Curtain*

Albrecht Dürer, *Hare*
Can you see the artist's famous initials and date – added over 500 years ago?

**Some artists have the amazing skill** of painting textures that look real enough to touch.

You can almost stroke the soft fur of this hare. Many of the brushstrokes are as thin as your own hair. Just look at those whiskers!

Try drawing contrasting lines, some thick and strong and others fragile and thin as a hair.

# Look – dream on

When you go to sleep, do you sometimes dream? Do you play games using your imagination? Are some of your memories especially vivid?

Marc Chagall found a wonderful way of bringing together his dream world, his imagination and his memories of real life. He put these together in magical pictures described as *music and poetry combined.*

Chagall painted many pictures for his wife Bella. This one shows the day when Bella brought food and flowers wrapped in shawls for his birthday. (You can see the embroidered shawls draped around the room and the birthday cake waiting on the table.) The artist started to paint, using warm colours to express his happiness. Suddenly he turned to kiss Bella. Chagall painted them **floating dreamily** up to the ceiling. They are head over heels in love.

What is your favourite memory? Try drawing it in a magical way.

Marc Chagall, *Birthday*

# Look – paint *is* the picture

You may think this is rather messy for a piece of great art. But if you think these trickles, spatters and puddles happened by accident, you would be wrong. The artist said, 'I can control the flow of paint, there is no accident'. He has not used paint to make a picture of something else. *Paint itself* is the picture!

Jackson Pollock liked to put his canvas on the floor and walk around it flinging, pouring and dripping paint across the surface. Sometimes he let the paint spill into gleaming puddles straight from the pot. At other times he pushed the paint around using stiff, dried-up brushes, sticks and trowels. He *drew* with paint.

This is called **action painting.** It's full of pattern, texture and energy. Don't you think the artist must have enjoyed this new way of making art?

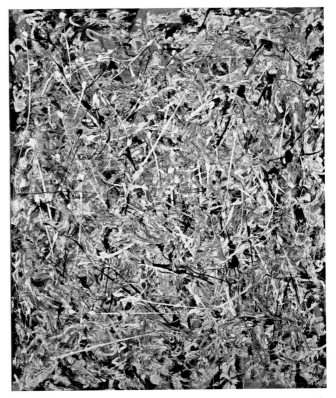

Jackson Pollock, *White Light*

Put some protective covering on the floor and try your own action painting!

# Look – does it exist?

**Artists often paint things that don't exist.**
You must have heard stories about fairies, elves and goblins. Giants, magical unicorns and strange half-human, half-animal creatures often appear in legends. We almost believe that these imaginary creatures exist because artists have painted such convincing pictures of how they look.

Paolo Uccello, *Saint George and the Dragon*

We all delight in the idea of **monsters, sea serpents and dragons.** In China, dragons are colourful, friendly, good-luck creatures. Yet we think of the poor old dragon as terrifying, scaly and wicked.

Here, a storm gathers as Saint George rides in on his white horse, just in time to rescue the princess from the dragon's terrible claws and teeth. Good triumphs over evil.

As you see, creatures which **don't exist** make exciting pictures!

In your mind you
can picture almost anything,
so design your very own
strange creature.

# *Look* – getting under the skin

## Artists investigate, just like detectives.

They want to find out about everything they see. They like to discover how things are made.

Artists have always studied the human skeleton to find out how bones fit together. Sometimes they even take dead creatures apart to learn more about the muscles, feathers or scales.

Have you ever had an x-ray picture taken in hospital? An x-ray is simply a photograph of what is *inside* you. Look at this coiled-up salt-water crocodile. It's been painted in **x-ray style** to show the reptile's insides. Follow its long, curving backbone with your finger and see how patterns decorate the spaces between the bones.

For Australian Aboriginal people this is a **magical crocodile** that lived long, long ago in a *billabong* (water-well). He ate his way through a vast mountain range to the sea and so created a great river.

Draw an orange as a ball shape. Draw it again and this time, draw the segments that you know are inside. Your x-ray picture will show the *structure* of the orange.

Yirawala, Namanjarwarre, *The Mardayin Crocodile*

25

Georges Seurat, *A Sunday on La Grande Jatte*

# Look – dotty idea!

This new style of painting once caused a shocking scandal. These days it doesn't surprise us at all. George Seurat's scientific experiments on how our eyes see colour are now famous.

Instead of mixing colours together, Seurat painted **thousands of tiny dots** of colour very close together. They *seem* to merge into each other, just as if they had been mixed together in the first place.

In this detail, you *think* you see a brown vest. In fact it is a mixture of red, purple, blue and yellow dots. These **mix in your eye** to look like brown.

Seurat also mixed white into all his colours. White is bright and gives a shimmery impression. His tiny dabs or points of colour add a lively texture to his pictures. This 'dotty' style of painting is called *pointillism*, and you can see why.

Make a completely dotty picture without any lines, using paint or felt-tip pens.

# Look – recycled for art

Have you ever collected anything, perhaps stones, shells, stamps or badges? Lay them out together to see how attractive they look.

Artists are always finding new ways to make art. This artist was a **treasure-hunter** who couldn't stop himself from hoarding oddments. He had an astonishing collection of ordinary and extraordinary things – stones, bones, shells, teeth, antlers, sticks, chains, rings, pearls, glitter, mirrors, glass eyes, beads, marbles, nails, screws, glass, broken china, gravel, coins, rope, letters, numbers and plastic shapes in bright colours.

He organised these in huge trays in his studio. Then he spread thick plastic glue mixed with paint on to a wood surface and pressed large objects, then smaller ones, into the glue. He stood on a chair to get a better view and rearranged the design over and over again.

His sparkling, glowing art helps us to see everyday bits and pieces in a completely new way. This is why seeing things through *an artist's eyes* is so important.

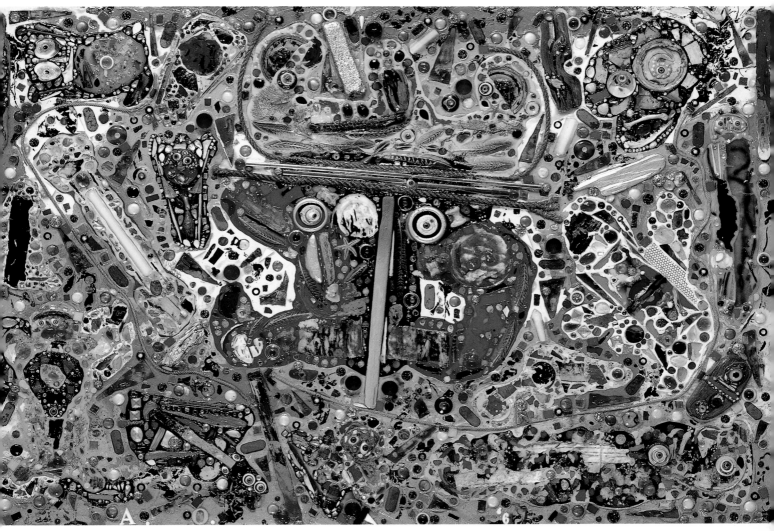

Alfonso Ossorio, *Balance*

Collect *all sorts* of interesting
bits and pieces. Lay them out
on a tray, ready to glue on your
own artwork.

Salvador Dali, *Paranoiac Face*

# *Look* – double meaning

double

A double image is a picture which can be seen as two different things, depending on how you look at it.

Painters have often invented double images – for example, a bowl of fruit that can also be seen as a face, or a gnarled tree that can also be seen as an old man. Some artists have become famous for cleverly making people see things in two ways.

Salvador Dali teases us with puzzling pictures that take us by surprise. He saw a photograph of African villagers sitting in the sun outside their home. The pattern created by the shapes inspired him to paint this ingenious picture. He even made it to be seen from two angles – like this, or as it is on the cover.

Artists use their skill to play with the way we look at things. We *enjoy* it when they *deceive* us with their brilliance.

Did you see the **double image** straight away? Show the picture to your friends, to test their reaction.

Can you draw an aged, twisted tree that also looks like the shape of a very old man?

# *Look* – every angle

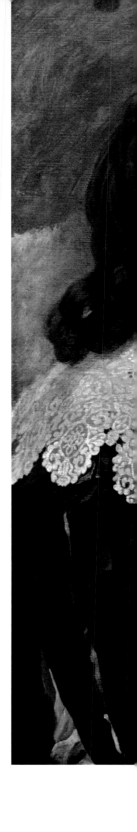

**Before photographs,** there were only portraits to show what someone looked like.

Often, people who had their portrait painted wanted the artist to make them look more handsome or beautiful than they really were. Others wanted the artist to show off how wealthy or important they were. Only the very best artists were chosen to paint kings and queens.

King Charles's Queen wanted to have her husband's likeness carved in marble. The **difficulty** was that the most famous sculptor at the time lived in Italy and the king lived in England.

How could the sculptor possibly know what the king really looked like? The solution was to ask Van Dyck to paint the king's head in three positions for an **all-round** view.

This painting gave the sculptor enough information to make a carving of King Charles that everyone agreed was **a most excellent likeness.**

Sir Antony Van Dyck, *Charles I in Three Positions*

Try drawing someone from
three different views:
side face, front face, then
the trickier three-quarter face,
just as in this painting.

# *Look* – storytelling

You probably have a favourite storybook with pictures illustrating what the story is about. The pictures help you to enjoy the story even more.

Artists often paint **story pictures**. There are no words in a painting, so you have to work out what each part of the picture means to discover the full meaning.

You can see that this picture is about an old man and an old woman. **The artist tells you their story** by painting the memories inside their heads. They look at each other and remember what

they were like when they were young. As a young man, he used to play his guitar and sing love songs to her when she was a beautiful young woman. She would run out to meet him when she heard his music.

The goblet between them is the cup of life. This one is filled with a golden light because they lived their life well. Despite their great age, they still see themselves as the loving couple they once were.

Can you draw or paint a story without words? Ask a friend to work out what your picture is saying.

Octavio Ocampo, *Forever Always*

Roy Lichtenstein, *Blam*

Make a comic-strip story
in four or five squares.
Use bright colours and black
outlines to make it look as if
it has been printed.

# Look – by hand or MACHINE ?

## If you think this looks like a printed picture

from a comic, you would be right. After all, how could all those dots be exactly the same if they had been painted by hand? All the shapes have perfect edges. Not a brushstroke can be seen. Even the black outlines look like printing ink. Yet, surprisingly, it was all painted **by hand!**

Pictures in comics, papers or magazines are made up from hundreds of tiny coloured dots so close you hardly notice them. Roy Lichtenstein brilliantly exaggerated this idea in his paintings.

## How did he do it? Masking tape

protected the sleek outlines of his shapes so that he never went over the edges.

He placed a piece of metal screen with round holes punched through it on the canvas. Then he used a *toothbrush* to brush colour into all the holes so that they looked identical, just as if they had been printed.

Lichtenstein's pictures are about love and romance as well as science fiction and battles. He brought a lot of *fun* into serious art.

# Look – even COMPUTERS do it

Most world-famous art in museums and galleries was created long before computers existed, much of it before there were modern machines of any sort. Things are different now. Computers are changing the way many artists work.

This is not a painting. It is computer – or digital – art, by a Japanese scientist who specialises in art that does strange things to your eyes.

Stare at these shapes for a moment. Can you see how the six white centre circles seem to 'buzz'? After a while your eyes begin to feel odd. The whole picture *shimmers* with movement.

Now gaze at the blank white spaces on the page and you will see the same design of circles again – this time only in white.

Computers offer an exciting new way of making art. One day, when you begin to be creative with computer design programmes, you will also discover wonderful ways with digital art.

Over to you.
Be bold and unafraid.
Experiment with art. One day,
you might even find new ways to teach
the world to see, just as artists have
always done throughout history.

Akiyoshi Kitaoka, *Rokuyo Stars*

# *Look* it up

Here you can find out more about the art and artists in this book, including when the paintings were made, when the artists lived, and where you can see the paintings.

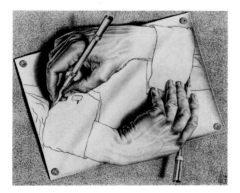

pages 8-9
## Drawing Hands, 1948
Maurits Cornelius Escher (1898–1972)

Escher, a Dutch artist was a master printer, a mathematician, a photographer and an architect. His unusual choice of subject matter surprises us and sometimes appears weird. His brilliance is in making highly complicated designs that show a mixture of the real and the unreal. His art plays with the way our eyes see and our brains understand the world.

pages 10-11
## The Chariot Race, c. 1882
Alexander Von Wagner (1838–1919)
*Manchester Art Gallery, Manchester, UK*

Von Wagner, a German artist, specialised in huge paintings telling the story of famous historical events. He skilfully recreated episodes from the past and showed what the architecture of a much earlier time would have looked like. He vividly captured the dramatic atmosphere of spectacular events.

pages 12-13
## Going up Garroby Hill, 2000
David Hockney (born 1937)
*Private Collection*

David Hockney is a famous English painter, a notable printmaker, a photographer and a stage designer. He was the most popular British painter of the 20th century. He experiments endlessly with new ideas and techniques. His huge amount of artwork is wide-ranging in style and astonishing in its variety.

back cover and pages 14-15
## Portrait of a Man, 1645-50
Isaac Fuller (1606?–72)
*Dulwich Picture Gallery, London, UK*

We know little about this British artist except that he was a flamboyant character who lived a wild life. He was a good teacher and produced the first British 'Drawing Book'. His confident painting was fiercely free in style. He painted a church altarpiece that was described in John Evelyn's diary as 'too full of nakeds for a chapel'!

page 16
## Still Life with a Flower Garland and a Curtain, 1658
Adriaen van der Spelt (1630–73) and Frans van Mieris (1635–81)
*The Art Institute of Chicago, Chicago, USA*

Very little is known about Adriaen van der Spelt. His talent was in *tromp l'oeil* painting, a technique that seeks to trick the eye by making things look real. In their still life paintings many Dutch artists revived an interest in this skill.

Frans van Mieris was a successful and prosperous Dutch painter who was particularly good at painting textures, especially of rich and brightly coloured shiny satins and silks.

page 17
## Hare, 1502
Albrecht Dürer (1471–1528)
*Albertina, Vienna, Austria*

Dürer produced a huge number of prints, paintings and drawings and also wrote books. He is the supreme master of printmaking. He was always curious about animals and would travel a long way to see an unusual one. He died when he caught a fever on an expedition to see a stranded whale.

## pages 18-19
### Birthday, 1915
Marc Chagall (1887–1985)
*Museum of Modern Art, New York, USA*

Chagall was one of nine children. His Russian family were members of a Jewish group which stressed the importance of prayer and miracles. His art is to do with his inner world where painting, poetry, music and imagination merge. His pictures have a dreamlike quality and many are love-songs to his beloved wife Bella.

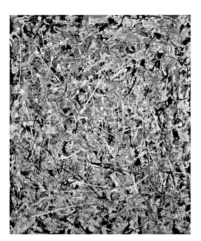

## pages 20-21
### White Light, 1954
Jackson Pollock (1912–56)
*Museum of Modern Art, New York, USA*

One of the great American artists, famous for his style of 'Action Painting'. Early on, Jackson Pollock painted murals and seascapes. Later, his 'dripping' technique gave him instant fame but he always denied that anything about his art was accidental. One art critic wrote, 'Pollack's talent is sumptuous, explosive, troubling' – and this sums up the sheer energy of his art.

## pages 22-23
### Saint George and the Dragon, c. 1470
Paolo Uccello (about 1397–1475)
*National Gallery, London, UK*

An Italian artist, Uccello was fascinated by the idea of perspective in painting. He and a few fellow artists experimented with how to make some things look near to the viewer and others further away, and how to show parts of the body coming forward or leaning back. This was the most exciting new development in painting almost 600 years ago!

## page 25
### Namanjawarre, the Mardayin Crocodile, c. 1973
Yirawala (1901/05–76)
*National Gallery of Australia, Canberra, Australia*

Aboriginal people lived in Australia long before Westerners settled there. Yirawala is an Aboriginal artist, one of the Kuninjka people from Arnhemland in the Northern Territory. His art explains 'The Dreaming', the Aboriginal way of describing how the world was created and how important the land is to them. Paintings were often done on tree bark using natural colours from earth and plants.

### pages 26-27
## A Sunday on La Grande Jatte, 1884-6
Georges Seurat (1859–91)
*The Art Institute of Chicago, Chicago, USA*

This French artist is famous for his experiments in the way we see colour and for his 'dotty' Pointilist technique. He abandoned earth colours for brighter ones better able to give the sparkling impression of natural light. He said, ' People say they see poetry in my painting but I see only science.'

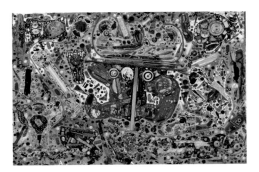

### pages 28-29
## Balance, 1961
Alfonso Ossorio (1916–90)
*Whitney Museum of American Art, New York, USA*

Ossario, an American artist, had a passion for collecting all kinds of everyday items. He saw the potential of found objects which he would saw, cut and paint in vivid colours before assembling them on his canvas. He called this artwork his 'Congregations'. He was keen for people to understand new art and generously devoted much time to promoting struggling artists.

### front cover and pages 30-31
## Paranoiac Face, c. 1935
Salvador Dali (1904–89)
*Private Collection*

An eccentric and flamboyant Spanish artist, Dali is one of the most original, unusual and popular painters of the 20th century. He is a master of optical trickery. He is called a Surrealist artist because his subjects are 'beyond real' and near to the world of dreams and nightmares. His fascinating pictures are full of visual surprises.

### pages 32-33
## Charles I in three positions, c. 1635
Sir Antony Van Dyck (1599–1641)
*The Royal Collection, Windsor, UK*

Van Dyck was a brilliant Belgian-born artist who painted masterpieces while still in his teens, when he was chief assistant to the great painter Rubens. He painted portraits, mythological and religious subjects. He is best remembered for his paintings of King Charles 1 and his court. His great skill is in painting portraits that reveal the personality of the sitter.

## Forever Always, 1989
pages 34-35
### Forever Always, 1989
Octavio Ocampo (born 1943)
*Private Collection*

This talented Mexican artist, who lives in the mountains near Mexico City, also studied acting, dancing, film and theatre. His special interest is in making pictures that have several meanings. The more you look, the more you can discover. Ocampo likes to lure the viewer with one overall image into seeing a second and third message within the same picture.

pages 36-37
### Blam, 1962
Roy Lichtenstein (1923–97)
*Yale University Art Gallery, Connecticut, USA*

Lichtenstein was a famous American 'Pop' artist. 'Pop' was the use of everyday popular subjects from modern life such as Donald Duck, washing machines and baked potatoes. Lichtenstein's big brash paintings are based on enlarged details from adverts and comic cartoons. His immediately recognisable style imitates printing techniques using strong colour, thick black lines and strong shapes which make a powerful impact.

page 39
### Rokuyo Stars, 2003
Akiyoshi Kitaoka (born 1961)
Digital Image

This Japanese artist is also a scientist who specialises in psychology – the way the brain understands the world. He is one of a new generation of artists who create computer-based digital art. He experiments with light, colour, movement and geometry in digital optical illusions. He also researches their effect on our eyes and brains. He calls his work 'Trick Eyes'.

# Index

Believe

Clever

Artful

Smart

talent

Trompe l'oiel

Craftsmanship

Entertaining

Skill

Brilliant

Puzzling

Otherworldly

Curious

Photographic

Optical illusion

Odd

Fooling

Real

Cheat

Inventive

Fake

Playful

Challenging

Expert

Persuade

Possible

Surprise

Sneaky